Helen's Big World

"We do not think with eyes
and ears, and our capacity
for thought is not measured
by five senses."

Helen's

written by DOREEN RAPPAPORT

illustrated by MATT TAVARES

Big World

The Life of Helen Keller

Disney · HYPERION
Los Angeles New York

For Jackie, Lyndie, Tara, and Wendy, four exceptional teachers

—D.R.

For Ava and Molly

—M.T.

ACKNOWLEDGMENTS: I thank the students of Mapleshade Elementary School, East Longmeadow, Massachusetts, and of Oak Grove Elementary School in Poughkeepsie, New York, for their insightful and truthful critiques of my book.

I thank Helen Selsdon, archivist at the American Foundation for the Blind, for sharing her invaluable insight and expertise.

In many instances, quotes by Helen Keller have been shortened without changing their meaning. Punctuation has been simplified. The quotes on pages 8–21 and 24–29 come from *The Story of My Life*; the quotes on pages 22–23 and 32–35 come from *The Radical Lives of Helen Keller*; the quotes on pages 2–3, 30–31, and 40–43 come from *Midstream*; the quotes on pages 36–37 are from *Helen Keller: A Life*; and those on pages 38–39 are from the American Foundation for the Blind website.

The Braille on the cover reads: Helen's Big World.

Text copyright © 2012 by Doreen Rappaport
Illustrations copyright © 2012 by Matt Tavares

Printed in Malaysia

First Hardcover Edition, October 2012
First Paperback Edition, May 2017
10 9 8 7 6 5 4 3 2 1
FAC-029191-17041

This book is set in 17-point Palatino LT Std/Monotype; Minion Pro/Fontspring; Caslon Antique Pro/Fontspring. The illustrations were created using watercolor, pencil, and gouache.

Library of Congress Control Number for Hardcover: 2011053516
ISBN 978-1-4847-4960-9
Visit www.DisneyBooks.com

AUTHOR'S NOTE

Researching and writing this biography of Helen Keller brought me back to when I was in elementary school and read about her for the first time. I remember when I went to the theater and saw the play *The Miracle Worker*, which focuses on the early relationship between Helen and Annie Sullivan. The most electrifying moment in the play, and in biographies of Helen Keller, was always the moment at the water pump, when Helen connected the water flowing over her hand with the word that Annie was spelling into her other hand. That moment reminds us of how we learn, and of the power of learning: the more we understand things, the larger our world becomes. Annie Sullivan opened up Helen Keller's limited, dark, silent world; it grew and grew until it truly became a big world.

Naturally curious, Helen gobbled up books and ideas and thought about everything she read. She formed opinions about what she believed needed to be changed to better our world, and didn't hesitate to say what she thought was important. She spoke out against child labor and for the right of women to vote when those ideas were still unpopular. She was often criticized for what she said, but she didn't stop speaking out. When I visit schools, I see children still reading and talking about Helen Keller. She remains an inspiration for all of us, for she reminds us that nothing is impossible if we put our mind to it.

—*DOREEN RAPPAPORT*

ILLUSTRATOR'S NOTE

When I first set out to illustrate this biography of Helen Keller, I was overwhelmed by the challenge of trying to visually capture the story of a person who could not see or hear. It seemed impossible. But the more I learned about her, I realized that maybe I was thinking about Helen Keller the wrong way. I was defining her by her deafness and blindness, but there was so much more to her story.

Helen Keller never saw the ocean or heard the sound of crashing waves. But she could feel the exhilaration of jumping in the water. She could ride in a sailboat, and feel the fluttering in her stomach as the sea rose and fell. She could taste the salty ocean spray, and feel the cold water as it splashed on her face. I kept this in mind as I illustrated this book, and tried to make sure my pictures focused on all the things she could do, instead of the two things she couldn't do.

The story of how she overcame her deafness and blindness is truly inspiring. But I think the real legacy of Helen Keller is how she made the most of what she had, and how she used the greatest gift of all, her mind, to try to understand the world and make it a better place.

—*MATT TAVARES*

Helen gurgled and giggled in her crib.
At six months, she crawled and said,
"How-d'ye," and "wah-wah," for *water.*
When she was one,
she ran after a ray of sunshine.
She loved the mockingbird's song
and the sweet smell of climbing roses.
But best of all was being on her father's lap
and in her mother's arms.

"The beginning of my life was simple and much like every other little life."

When Helen was nineteen months old,
an illness her doctors could not name struck her.
When she recovered,
she could no longer see or hear or speak.

When her parents pressed her close,
she knew their smell and touch.
But she could not see them or hear them
or say their names.

"In the dreary month of February
came the illness which
closed my eyes and ears.
Gradually, I got used to the silence
and darkness that surrounded me."

Helen tried to figure out
her dark, silent world.
She used her hands to recognize objects.
She used her brain to make up signs
to let her family know what she wanted.
Putting on pretend glasses meant *Father*.
Her hand on her cheek meant *Mother*.

But she could not make up enough signs
to have her needs understood.
Many times she screamed and kicked
and ended up sobbing.
Sometimes she hit the people she loved.

"My failures to make
myself understood
were followed by
outbursts."

When Helen was almost seven,
Annie Sullivan came to teach her.
Annie had been legally blind.
After several operations, she could see again.
But her eyes were still weak.

Annie gave Helen a doll and
with her fingers traced the letters
D-O-L-L on Helen's palm.
Helen thought Annie wanted the doll back,
so she kicked and screamed.
Annie gave Helen some cake
and traced C-A-K-E on Helen's palm.
Helen traced the letters back on Annie's palm.

Annie gave Helen many objects and
spelled their names with her fingers.

"I was interested in this finger play and tried to imitate it."

Helen imitated Annie's finger movements.
But she did not understand
that she was spelling words
or that things had names.

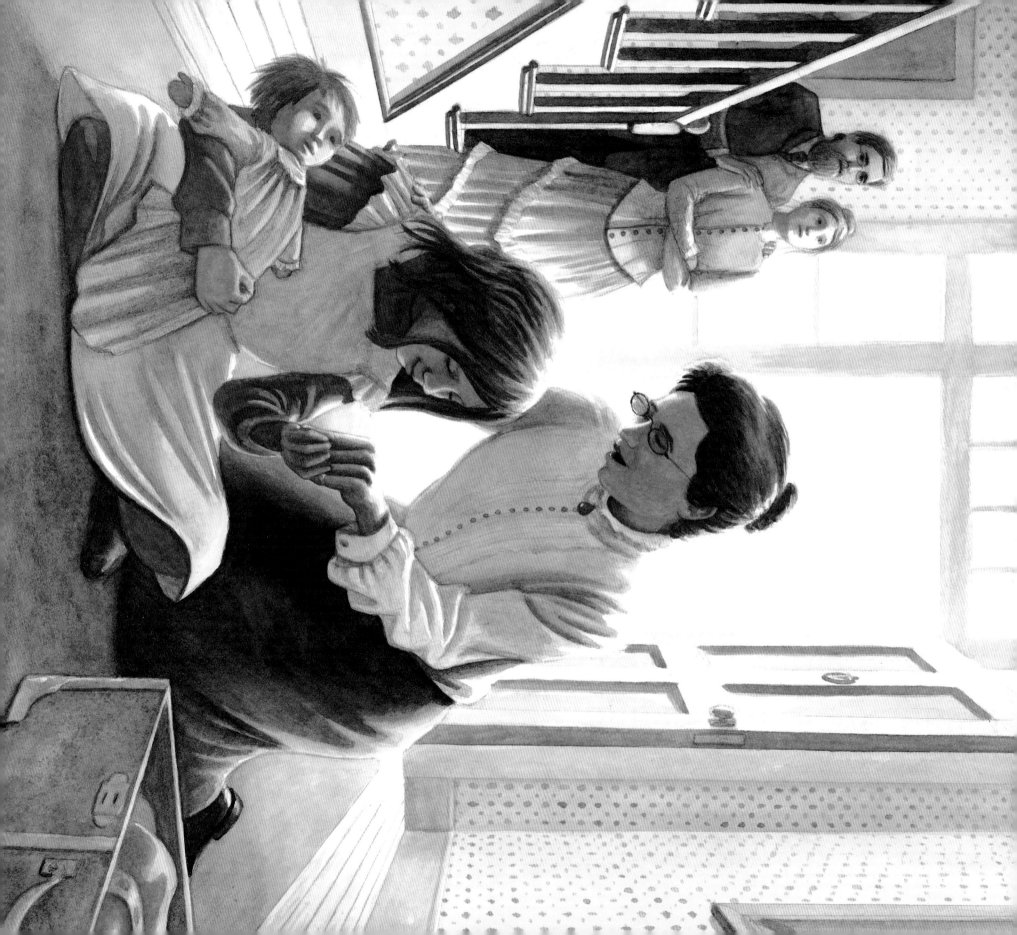

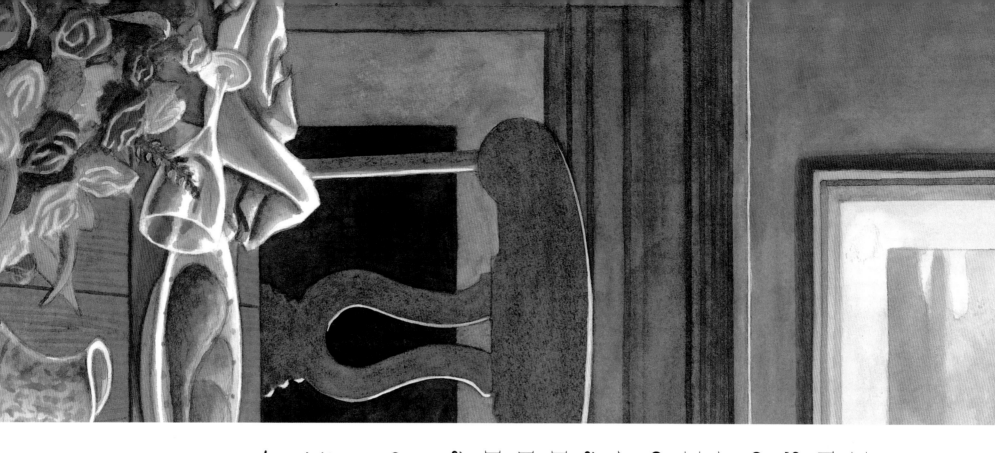

Helen liked the spelling game,
but she didn't like learning table manners.
She tried to eat with her fingers
off Annie's plate.
Annie wouldn't let her.
Helen screamed and threw her spoon
on the floor.
Annie forced Helen out of her chair
and made her pick it up.
Helen threw it on the floor again.
Back and forth they went, until
Helen finally used the spoon
and ate off her *own* plate.

**"In the still, dark world
in which I lived,
there was no tenderness."**

One day, a month later,
Annie pumped water into Helen's hand
and spelled W-A-T-E-R on her other palm.
As Helen felt the cold water,
she understood that Annie was spelling
the word *water*.
Her face lit up, and she spelled W-A-T-E-R
on Annie's palm again and again and again.

**"That living word
awakened my soul,
gave it light, hope, joy,
and set it free."**

Helen touched the water pump.
Annie spelled P-U-M-P on Helen's hand.
Then Helen touched Annie,
and Annie spelled T-E-A-C-H-E-R.

For the next few years,
Helen learned thousands of new words
and practiced speaking them with her fingers
from the second she woke up
until she went to sleep.

Annie also taught Helen
to see with her fingers.
Every day for many weeks,
Helen touched a lily growing in a pot.
She felt its pointy buds open
and form silky blossoms.
Helen smelled violets in Annie's hands,
and felt the warmth of the sun on her face.
And Annie spelled each new word or idea.

With her fingers, Helen felt
the vibrations of
a person laughing,
a chick bursting out of an egg,
a horse neighing,
and a baby pig squealing.
And Annie spelled each new word or idea.

"There is not a talent,
or an inspiration or joy in me
that has not been awakened
by her loving touch."

Annie placed paper on a writing board with grooves.
She showed Helen how to guide
her pencil with her left hand
as she wrote in the grooves with her right hand.
Once Helen learned to write,
she would not stop.

"July 12, 1887
Helen will write mother letter
papa did give helen medicine
teacher did give helen peach. . . . "

"January 9, 1888
Apples have no edges and no angles.
Apples grow on trees.
They grow in orchards.
When they are ripe, they fall on
the ground."

"January 29, 1889
Astronomer comes from the Latin
word astra, which means stars.
When we are sleeping quietly in our beds,
they are watching the beautiful sky
through the telescope.
The stars are called the earth's brothers
and sisters."

Helen learned so quickly,
some people called her a genius.
Other people said Annie was the genius.
Articles were written about Helen.
By the time she was eight,
she was famous.

Helen liked writing with a pencil.
She loved when Annie spelled books to her.
But she wanted to read books on her own,
so Annie taught her Braille.
Braille uses raised dots for letters and words.

Annie put pieces of cardboard
with raised dots on different objects.
She spelled words into Helen's hand
as Helen ran her fingers over the dots
and touched the objects.
More objects, more dots, more words.
Practice, practice—
until she read as quickly as sighted children.

"At first I had only
a few books in raised print.
I read them over and over,
until the words
were so worn and pressed
I could scarcely
make them out."

Annie took Helen
walking in the forest,
jumping in the salty ocean,
tobogganing down snowy hills,
bicycling in tandem,
and sailing in a boat.
And she spelled out each new experience.

"The wind rose,
and the waves chopped angrily.
Our little boat swirled in the billows,
only to be driven down
with angry howl and hiss.
Our hearts beat fast."

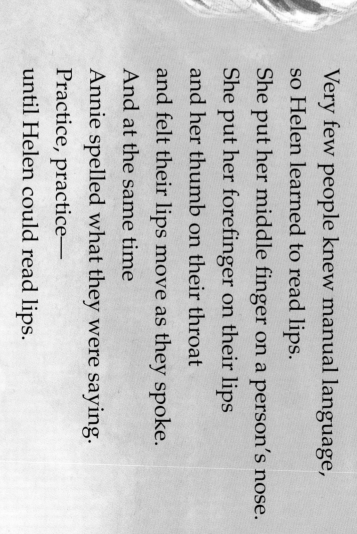

Very few people knew manual language,
so Helen learned to read lips.

She put her middle finger on a person's nose.
She put her forefinger on their lips
and her thumb on their throat
and felt their lips move as they spoke.

And at the same time
Annie spelled what they were saying.

Practice, practice—
until Helen could read lips.

Helen touched a person's face
and felt their lips and tongue vibrate.
Then she touched her own lips and tongue
and imitated what she had felt.

Practice, practice—
until she learned to speak.

"It was my ambition to speak
like other people.
We worked hard and faithfully,
yet we did not quite reach our goal."

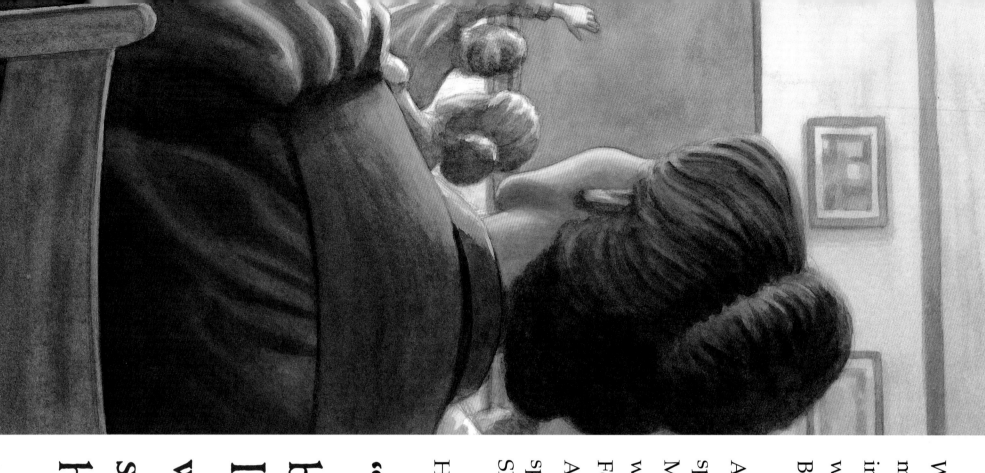

When Helen decided to go to college, most people said that it would be impossible for her to keep up with the work.

But she was determined.

Annie sat next to Helen in class, spelling what the teachers said. Most of the books Helen had to read were not in Braille.

For more than five hours a day, Annie read the books and spelled them to Helen. She hurt her eyes doing it.

Helen graduated with honors.

"Teacher read many books to me. In spite of repeated warnings from oculists, she has always abused her eyes for my sake."

While in college,
Helen wrote her autobiography.
She explained how Annie taught her.
The book was a great success.
People marveled at how much Helen knew
and what a wonderful teacher Annie was.

But some people questioned
how Helen could describe things that
she could not see or hear.
They did not understand that
she could smell lilacs and roses and
feel the golden rays of the sun on her face
and the soft, springy earth under her feet.

"I have the advantage of
a mind trained to think,
and that is the difference
between myself and most
people, not my blindness
and their sight."

Helen read all kinds of books
and met all kinds of people and
thought about all kinds of things
and spoke out about
what was important to her.

She spoke against war
and against child labor.
She spoke for workers' unions,
and for the right of women to vote
and for justice for black Americans.

Many people did not like her ideas.
Helen believed that words brought freedom,
and she would not be silenced.

"I do not like
the world as it is;
so I am trying
to make it a little more
as I would like it."

The sign reads:

INTRODUCING
THE 8TH WONDER
OF THE WORLD
HELEN KELLER

Helen starred in a movie about her life.

She didn't like that very much.

But she did like being onstage.

The audience asked questions.

Annie spelled the questions

on Helen's palm,

and Helen answered them.

Sometimes Helen was funny.

"Does Miss Keller think of marriage?"

"Yes. Are you

proposing to me?"

Sometimes she was serious.

"Do you think women should go

into politics?"

"Yes, if they want to."

Some people felt sad

that Helen was performing.

But she needed the money,

and she felt good earning it.

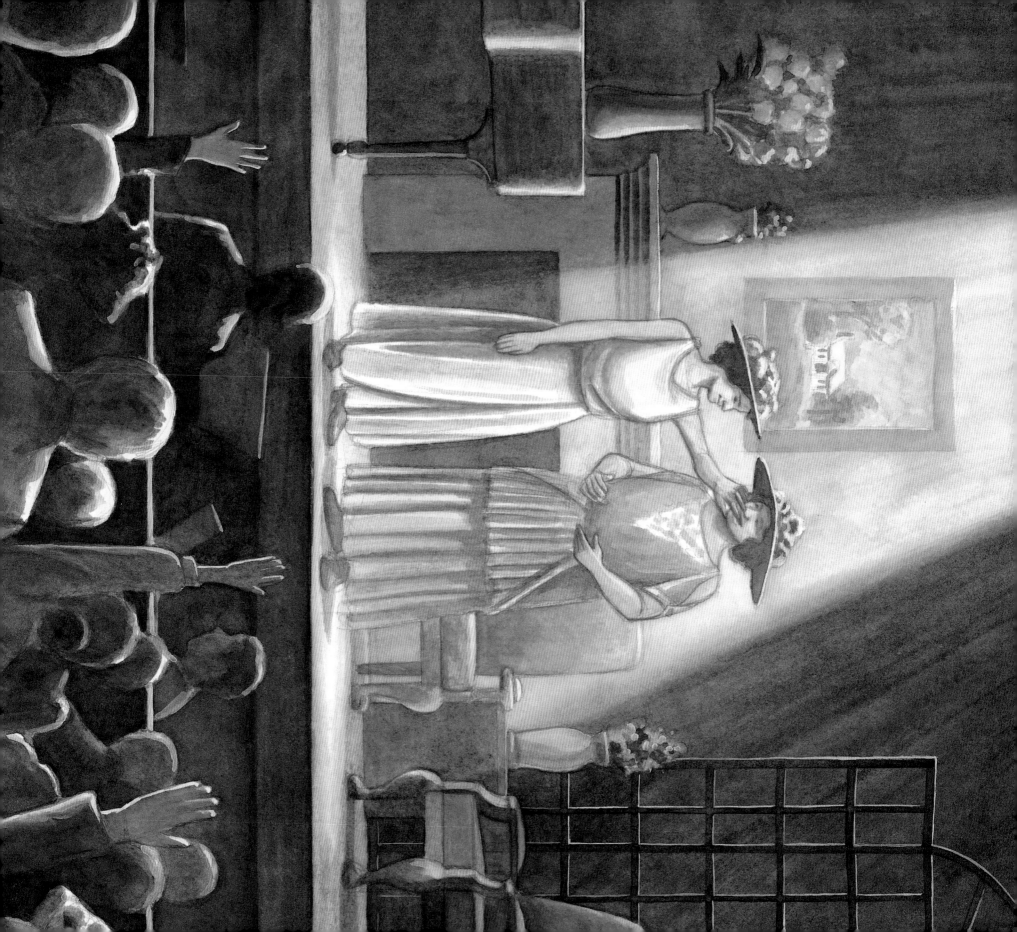

Helen traveled all over the world,
giving talks on the needs of blind people.
She spoke in people's homes and in large halls.
She met with lawmakers and teachers and presidents.
She insisted that eye doctors examine newborns.
She insisted there be more books in Braille
and better education and meaningful work
for people with disabilities.

"The chief handicap of the blind is not blindness, but the attitude of seeing people toward them."

For forty-nine years, Annie
was at Helen's side,
wherever she went,
helping her do the things
she could not do by herself.

Annie's health weakened.
She died when Helen was fifty-six.

**"I often wonder
what my life
would have been like
if she had not
come into it."**

Polly Thomson was there to help Helen,
but some people wondered
how Helen would survive without Annie.

Helen used the strength and knowledge that Annie had taught her to face the world.

She kept traveling and speaking, always saying what she thought was important, until she died at the age of eighty-seven.

"I love my country. But my love for America is not blind. Perhaps I am more conscious of her faults because I love her so deeply."

IMPORTANT DATES

June 27, 1880: Helen Adams Keller is born in Tuscumbia, Alabama.

February 1882: Helen gets sick and becomes deaf and blind.

March 1887: Annie Sullivan becomes Helen's teacher.

February 1888: She learns to read in Braille.

Spring 1890: Helen begins speech lessons.

October 1894-1896: Helen and Annie move to New York City, where Helen attends the Wright-Humason School for the Deaf.

August 29, 1896: Helen's father, Arthur H. Keller, dies.

October 1896: Helen prepares for college at the Cambridge School for Young Ladies.

1900-1904: Helen attends Radcliffe College.

1903: Her autobiography, *The Story of My Life*, is published.

1909: Helen begins to speak out on issues other than her life, such as women's rights, socialism, unions, birth control, civil liberties, and justice for black Americans.

1914: Polly Thomson comes to work for Helen and Annie.

1919: Helen stars in *Deliverance*, a silent movie about her life.

1919-1923: Helen and Annie perform in vaudeville.

June 1921: Helen's mother, Kate Adams Keller, dies.

1924: Helen is hired by the American Foundation for the Blind as a fund-raiser and speaker.

1924-1954: Helen travels the world, visiting over thirty-five countries.

October 20, 1936: Annie Sullivan Macy dies. Polly Thomson assumes Sullivan's role.

1953: *The Unconquered*, a documentary film about Helen's life, is released.

1957: *The Miracle Worker*, a play about Helen's life, opens on Broadway.

1961: Helen suffers a stroke and retires from public life.

1964: She receives the Presidential Medal of Freedom.

June 1, 1968: Helen Keller dies in her sleep.

Selected Research Sources

Braddy, Henney, Nella. *Anne Sullivan Macy: The Story Behind Helen Keller.* Garden City, N.Y.: Doubleday, Doran, 1933.

Einhorn, Lois J. *Helen Keller, Public Speaker: Sightless but Seen, Deaf but Heard.* Westport, Conn.: Greenwood Press, 1998.

Herrmann, Dorothy. *Helen Keller: A Life.* New York: Alfred A. Knopf, 1998.

Keller, Helen. *Helen Keller, Her Socialist Years: Writings and Speeches.* New York: International Publishers, 1967.

————. *Light in My Darkness.* West Chester, Pa.: Swedenborg Foundation Press, 2000.

————. *Midstream: My Later Life.* Garden City, N.Y.: Doubleday, Doran, 1929.

————. *Out of the Dark: Essays, Lectures, and Addresses on Physical and Social Vision.* Garden City, N.Y.: Doubleday, Page & Company, 1920.

————. *The Song of the Stone Wall.* New York: The Century Company, 1910.

————. *The Story of My Life.* With supplementary accounts by Anne Sullivan and John Albert Macy; edited with a new foreword and afterword by Roger Shattuck with Dorothy Herrmann. New York: Norton, 2003.

————. *Teacher: Anne Sullivan Macy.* Garden City, N.Y.: Doubleday, 1955.

Lash, Joseph P. *Helen and Teacher: The Story of Helen Keller and Anne Sullivan Macy.* New York: Delacorte Press, 1980.

Nielsen, Kim E. *The Radical Lives of Helen Keller.* New York: New York University Press, 2004.

If you would like to learn more about Helen Keller, you can read:

Cline-Ransome, Lesa. *Helen Keller: The World in Her Heart.* New York: HarperCollins, 2008.

Dash, Joan. *The World at Her Fingertips: The Story of Helen Keller.* New York: Scholastic, 2002.

DuBois, Muriel. *Helen Keller: A Photo-Illustrated Biography.* North Mankato, Minn.: Capstone Press, 2005.

Koestler-Grack, Rachel A. *The Story of Helen Keller.* New York: Facts on File, 2009.

Lakin, Patricia. *Helen Keller and the Big Storm.* New York: Aladdin, 2001.

Lawlor, Laurie. *Helen Keller: Rebellious Spirit.* New York: Holiday House, 2001.

MacLeod, Elizabeth. *Helen Keller: A Determined Life.* Tonawanda, N.Y.: Kids Can Press, 2004.

Sullivan, George E. *Helen Keller.* New York: Scholastic, 2001.

Websites:

American Foundation for the Blind (www.afb.org) has great resources if you follow the Braille Bug link.

Manual Language Chart

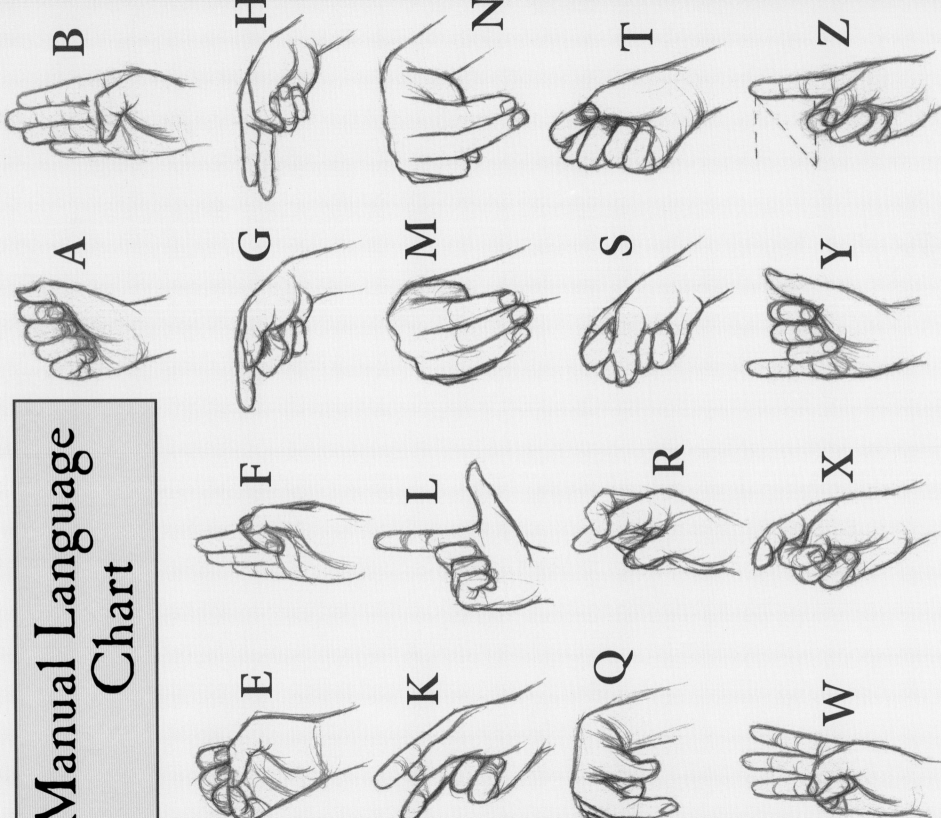

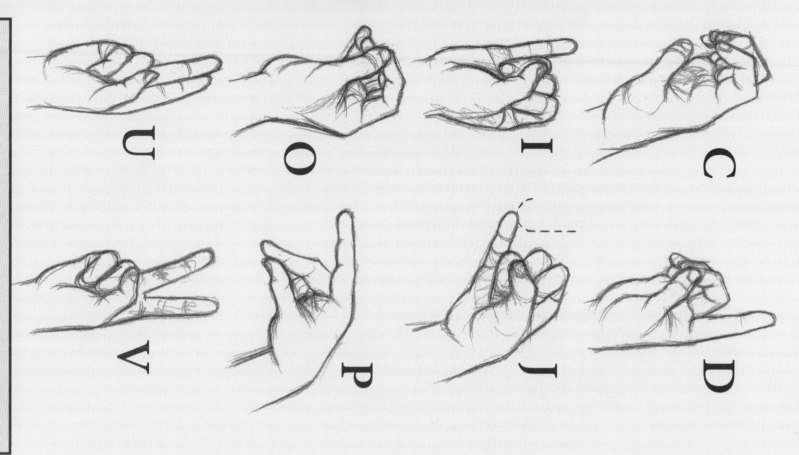

This is the alphabet Annie Sullivan taught Helen Keller so that they could communicate with each other. Placing her hand within Helen's, Annie would make letter shapes to form words—and words lead to ideas!